BELLWETHER MESSAGES

2013 Savant Poetry Anthology

EDITED BY DANIEL S. JANIK

Savant Books and Publications
Honolulu, HI, USA
2013

Published in the USA by Savant Books and Publications
2630 Kapiolani Blvd #1601
Honolulu, HI 96826
http://www.savantbooksandpublications.com

Printed in the USA

Edited by Daniel S. Janik
Cover Art and Design by Daniel S. Janik

13-digit ISBN: 9780988664043
10-digit ISNB: 0988664046

Dedication

It is my pleasure to dedicate this 2013 Anthology of
Poetry to the millions of poetry lovers out there who
regularly peruse the myriad literary beaches for poetic
flotsam and jetsam in the hope of discovering a treasure.
In discovering our fourth annual Savant Anthology of
Poetry, BELLWETHER MESSAGES, I believe you have
done just that.

Take off your constricting shoes, roll up your pant legs,
and allow yourself to drift from one poem to the next,
wiggling your toes into the words, and letting their
meaning ooze into your every pore.

It's been a challenge to sort through the literally hundreds
of this year's entries, but it is my hope that this anthology
brings you what I hope you will agree is the very best of
this years poetic treasures.

- Daniel S. Janik 2013

Table of Contents

Two Poems by Shawn P. Canon   1

Three Poems by Natascha Hoover   7

Three Poems by IKO   21

Two Poems by Daniel S. Janik   29

Three Poems by Vivekanand Jha   39

Three Poems by Thomas Koron   49

Two Poems by Doc Krinberg   57

A Poem by Cathal Patrick Little   63

A Poem by Uhene'   69

A Poem by Peter Mallett   77

Three Poems by Tender Bastard   83

Three Poems by Emma Myles   97

A Poem by Ken Rasti   109

Three Poems by Ashley Vaughan   115

Bellwether Messages

Two Poems by Shawn P. Canon

Bits & Peaces is the Music, Art & Poetry in Motion of Shawn P. Canon from 1968 to the present.

This was written during the 1968-1969 Viet Nam Campaigns with the U.S. Army 268th Combat Aviation.

I dedicate this to my parents Feliciano and Betty S. Canon...May They Rest In Peace.

An Incidental Reverie

350 of the Julian Calendar

Aggregated amongst volumes of technical lanes
Segregates my side of the fence with Big Brother.
If by some enchanting jest of Merlins's legerdemain
I would transmute every manuscriptual bother
Into realms of melodious gleams...
Namely Country, Blues, Jazz and Classics (the mother).

Bits & Peaces

This was written during the 1968-1969 Viet Nam
Campaigns with the U.S. Army 268th Combat Aviation.

I dedicate this to my parents Feliciano and Betty S.
Canon…May They Rest In Peace.

Paradox of Human Baboons

Two days later

I saw an idiot who scorned bald-headed priests.
Conversely, it makes me wonder
Of people that hoot at long-haired freaks.
Should they stop and think not to blunder
The fact that they too appear quite a flaunter
For being narrow-minded mice.

Bits & Peaces

Bellwether Messages

Three Poems by Natáscha Hoover

In her own quirky and irreverent style, poet Natáscha Hoover, shares her darkly adventurous thoughts with readers. Prompted by deeply-felt memories of early years spent in Hawai'i, living with an unstable mother, Natáscha delivers poetry inspired by everything she observes as she seeks to reflect the deeper layers of ordinary experiences.

Bellwether Messages

A Drowned Balloon

In the frigid Pacific
A top-heavy gypsy
Once full of fire
And hot air
Now only full of color
Now stringy
Drawn out & wet
Beholden to the currents.

She just floats along
The colors ever changing
She has a swishy sound...
Yes, she makes a sound.

On top of the waves
Above the waves
Weightless & suffocating
At the same time...
all the same.

Like she is screaming.

First red
Then yellow
Then blue

Then green
Whatever her hue,
She is turning, churning…
And turning

Turned by the salt
Then the rain
Then the fish…
She retains her swish.

And the basket,
Once light with cargo,
Is slowly disintegrating
One.
Splinter.
At.
A.
Time…
Like life splinters off
Piece by peace…

The bodies long ago…
Eaten.

She is chewed by life
Teeming in the seas.
The first to go

…Are the Eyes
…Then the brows
…Then the heart
…Then the blood;
Everyone takes a bit
…Then the mind
…Then the soul
As she drinks the salty sea
…Gulping
…Then swallowing…
Forgotten are her colors
And her strings
And her flags
And her basket
--Once full of fruit--
Which swings
…And swims

Back & forth
Back
And
Forth
Back
And
Forth.

"Where is the fourth man?" she asks.

"I don't need anyone
To save me."
And because one doesn't even need a boat
(because THAT is just
A vessel.)
All one needs is a spirit
Or at least
…spirituality
For God's sake!
Such an ache!
To set oneself adrift
…After adrifting

You are,

Only one,
Of the many 'Anothers'
Pushing all away,
…and saving yourself
Pushing them out of the basket, really
(Before the basket
Hits the water)
Because who would be
Dangled?
Up with me?
(One so unworthy?)
With someone so swarthy

…At least in a non-leaky boat
…Or at least seaworthy
Me, without a lead collar
…Or a woolen bag
…Cinched at the neck
Like some supposed witch?
Or a captured trophy fish
…that was wrestled with
…for hours.

Walking along Kinau Street one evening, where there are no cherry blossom trees, the writer was inspired by some smashed pink flowers she saw on the sidewalk, near Foodland.

Cherry Blossom Pancakes

Poems are like Cherry Blossom Pancakes
...which I don't eat.

My mind is like a tree
and the flowers fall off
one by one...
or in bunches...
leaving my branches
...bare and nude
...after being flipped by my brain...
until the next Bloom.

Except my cherry blossoms
are yellow and flat...
jacked
and look sick on the vine
...until they hit the ground
...and make a sound
(like I've dropped something)
but
...I have not.
...where they are jolted to another color
...another dimension, really.
I cannot perceive
But vaguely sense

Its existence
At least, they, a little bit rhyme
THERE.

And there
…I sweep them up in arms
one at a time
and burn them
…into compost.

Bellwether Messages

The Warrior

Trying to block off
My emotional war with my over-sized samurai helmet

Tottering side to side on my head
This way and that
Ruthlessly
Left to right
Then left
As I make my way through
The bamboo forest
Purposefully
Dutifully.

The rings of the bark of
These tall weed structures
Hypnotizing and confusing
Me
to unlawful things
For the sake of Peace.

Where is Kurosawa now?

Bellwether Messages

Three Poems by IKO

Born in Europe, IKO traveled westward towards a warm and wonderful climate. She has been a university and college instructor of foreign languages, an entrepreneur, a translator (French, German and English), and an artist. When not spending her time pursuing an active outdoor lifestyle, IKO reads copiously, especially in her areas of interest: philosophy (both Eastern and Western traditions) and the many fascinating religious traditions of our world. Balancing this combination of active and esoteric, IKO believes that the ambiance of Hawaii corresponds to the harmony of her family life.

Quo Vadis

This morning I watched balloons,
delight of last night,
tiredly circling the floor.
Here and there they sat,
but two, one purple, one blue,
furtively touched ever so gently
trembling, aquiver,
encircled,
enmeshed their ties,
enlaced, embraced.
while others sat contentedly
in a corner, on the floor
awaiting their destiny.

Do they choose, do they know?
Do we choose-do we know?

Bellwether Messages

My will for you

Sometimes i wish to give you all i have—
my house. it is but lent to me,
my car will be no good for you.
all my things
might burn
might rot
might disintegrate

but i wish to give you a pledge, something of me—
let me see, what do i own?
my body, my soul, my spirit...
i own but my time. and that I will to you, my love,
with all my heart.

Bellwether Messages

Sleepless, dreamless nights

Looking, searching,
looking, searching
what, how, who, when, if?
words jumble—
chaos
ideas tumble—
what if
what if
what if—

ocean, moon, stars,
waves, light,
delight—
I pray it may last—
but what if?
what if?

Looking for refuge in the solace of dreams,
searching in the night—
what if...?

Two Poems by Daniel S. Janik

Daniel S. Janik is a multi-award winning poet, author, songwriter and producer. His collected poems currently appear in three volumes: FOOTPRINTS, SMILES AND LITTLE WHITE LIES (Savant 2008), THE ILLUSTRATED MIDDLE EARTH (Savant 2008), LAST AND FINAL HARVEST (Savant 2008), various Savant Poetry Anthologies and numerous other publications. He has authored two curiosity-based, discovery-driven transformative children's books, A WHALE'S TALE (Savant, 2008), and THE TURTLE DANCES (Savant, in press). His pioneering educational book, UNLOCK THE GENIUS WITHIN (Rowman and Littlefield Education, 2005) will soon go into a second edition. *Clean Water, Common Ground* (National Film Network, 1999), his documentary on the state of the earth's water received two Telly awards and is available through the National Film Network.

Danny's Song (1992)

Alone I live, but with my past,
A partner who holds to me fast.
Images of a childhood boy
Left behind without the joy
That children and most parents hold
Close to their hearts like precious gold.
The warm past comes, but then it goes,
Buried beneath the frozen snow.

Once-jump, twice-abound,
Sunlight patches on dark ground,
The kangaroos go hopping by,
Waving paws with tails held high.

The wish that was, is naught again,
But nothing asked, then nothing gained.
Call upon the heart's delight
To find new treasures in the night.
Hey, there, little one within
It's not all over, just begin.
Hold fast your love with all you might,
Bring back the past within your sight.

Once-jump, twice-abound,
Sunlight patches on dark ground,

The kangaroos go hopping by,
Waving paws with tails held high.

Remember birthdays, joy and song,
They're what you're searching for my son.
The touch, the voice, the soft caress
Of kindness, love without duress.
A place to curl up safe within,
The loving arms you thought to win,
Little child, that secret place
Is always there in my embrace.

Once-jump, twice-abound,
Sunlight patches on dark ground,
The kangaroos go hopping by,
Waving paws with tails held high.

Bellwether Messages

Danny's Song (2000)

Underneath the clear blue sky,
The little children play.
They laugh and shout and run about
All through the sunshine days.

All good things 'neath sky are found
Upon this lovely planet earth,
So blue and green and round.

Underneath a big green tree
The little birdies sing.
They chirp so sweet, and stamp their feet,
While fluffing pretty wings.

All good things 'neath sky are found
Upon this lovely planet earth,
So blue and green and round.

Underneath the waves in streams
The little turtles swim.
they hide and seek, and play and squeak,
With little turtle grins.

All good things 'neath sky are found
Upon this lovely planet earth,

So blue and green and round.

Safe atop the lily pads,
The little froggies croak,
Then jump -- kersplash! -- and laugh and laugh,
And show their bright green coats.

All good things 'neath sky are found
Upon this lovely planet earth,
So blue and green and round.

Underneath delicious silvery waves,
Little fishies swim.
They somersault and dart about
And flash their silver fins.

All good things 'neath sky are found
Upon this lovely planet earth,
So blue and green and round.

Afar beneath the deep blue sea,
The little dolphins play.
They jump the waves in ceaseless ways,
All through the stormy days.

All good things 'neath sky are found
Upon this lovely planet earth,

So blue and green and round.

Underneath a big, round moon,
The kangaroos abound.
They dance about, while holding tails,
In circles round and round.

All good things 'neath sky are found
Upon this lovely planet earth,
So blue and green and round.

Underneath the covers warm,
Little children sleep.
And dream of fish and frogs and things
While all the world's at peace.

All good things 'neath sky are found
Upon this lovely planet earth,
So blue and green and round.

Bellwether Messages

Three Poems by Vivekanand Jha

Dr. Vivekanand Jha is a translator, editor and award winning poet from India. He is Diploma in Electronics and Communication Engineering, Certificate in Computer Hardware and Networking, MA and Ph. D in English. He is a contributing poet to Wavelengths – 2011 Savant Anthology of Poetry (USA) which has won first place in the 2011 London Book Festival. He has been Poetry Contest Winner-Third Place Winner for the poem "Hands Heave to Harm and Hamper" conducted by Beginners®, a documentary, graphic, nonfiction book series (USA). His poem, "Song of Woes" was featured in the 10 Selected Poems for Performance & 10 Selected Poems for Award in 2nd Korea-Nigeria Poetry Feast on 21st March 2012 organized by the Korean Cultural Centre Nigeria. He is the author of five books of poetry. He has also edited nine critical anthologies on Indian English Novels. His works have been published in more than eighty five magazines round the world. Besides his poems have been chosen and published in more than twenty poetry anthologies. He has more than twenty-five research and critical articles published in various national and international anthologies and referred journals. He is son of noted professor, poet and award winning translator Dr. Rajanand Jha (Crowned with Sahitya Akademi Award, New Delhi).

Bellwether Messages

Disposal

I beseeched the Lord for serenity;
he granted me the solitude of sadness.

I craved for a longevity;
he filled my seemingly endless life full of failures,
furies and frustration.

I solicited Him to teach me something about
figures of speech;
he taught irony, pun and satire.

I implored Him to show me the way to success;
he guided me along a prosperous path that ended
in a blind alley.

I entreated Him to bless me with a bride belle:
He granted me a mate of blunted wit,
a womb sterile, swelled with pride, shaking with
disease,
infamous in notoriety, easy in virtue.

I suddenly awoke and realized
that asking anything from the Lord
is like a bartering in the marketplace:
bargaining terms and conditions apply.

I decided to leave all to the Lord;
He bestowed on me what, unknown to me, I
required.

Bellwether Messages

To Death

I snatched myself from your brutal jaws
all prepared to pulverize me.

I can't counsel others,
so I have cultivated a cult to deal with you:

Your icy hands can frost the blood bolting through
my veins,
but not the ink bubbling in my brain.

You can kill your creation,
but not my creativity.

You can mutilate my mortal mass,
but not the inscription of my immortality
that I would carve and whittle
with the tip of talent before I die.

Fear of death I bid you good bye!

Three Poems by Thomas Koron

Thomas Koron was born in Grand Rapids, Michigan on May 19, 1977. He has attended Grand Rapids Community College, Aquinas College and Western Michigan University. He remains active in Grand Rapids as a writer, composer and performer.

This poem is dedicated to Michelle Albright.

Black Satin

Upon the sheets my sultry mistress lies,
As she welcomes me her room to enter,
With soft candles reflecting in her eyes.
She rolls her body over the center;
Her skin is soft—her hair gently flowing—
As I lean down and give her lips a kiss.
We embrace throughout the night, and knowing
Come the daylight the warmth we both shall miss.
And then, she whispers in my ear so sweet,
"Please come to me again, my music man."
Time grants another chance for us to meet
At nightfall here, or at least, shall we plan?
Life moves in directions mysterious,
And leaves us bewildered and curious.

Bellwether Messages

Snapdragon

I found pleasure in every direction,
As I wandered mystified through the fields.
A snapdragon captured my attention;
Possessed with the sensation that it yields.
Moving slowly over the grass, I feel
Entranced; the flower holds me in a daze.
Once the snapdragon's near, I stop and kneel;
And then, dream into the bright summer haze.
How I had gone for many miles without
The joyful zest, which now flows through my soul.
Shedding away feelings of fear and doubt,
With enchantment that makes my spirit whole.
Surrounded by colors of brilliant red,
I make that velvety garden my bed.

Bellwether Messages

The Veil of the Night

At dusk we shall bask in the veil of night,
Covering all that the eye ever sees.
A cloak of clouds masking the moon so bright,
As bats fly in circles above the trees.
We push our problems so far out of sight,
Searching for peace, we set our minds at ease.
Until we rise up with the morning light,
Hoping that we've rested enough to please.
We go to sleep putting our lives on hold,
Bringing a sense of calmness to our dreams.
Relaxed at last, we sleep the night away,
But there are stars with stories to be told.
They keep us company, or so it seems,
And then, they disappear into the day.

Bellwether Messages

Two Poems by Doc Krinberg

Doc Krinberg grew up in California where he had numerous jobs to include taxi driver, strip club barker, and a career as a Navy Diver. With a doctorate in education, he now teaches and resides in Virginia.

...again, to Laura, E Hoomau Maua Kealoha

A Lover...

I sway a tall palm
You, like Kukaniloko
Under me fertile
Laying one leg up
Taste cut melon in my mouth
Honey leg soft sweet

...*again, to Laura,* E Hoomau Maua Kealoha

For an Aging Helen

Eyes a horizon
Fading iris like sunset
Not getting younger

Brass rings out of reach
Corners of your eyes walked on
Doors shutting slowly

Look in your mirror
Childhood remembered and
The future forgotten

A Poem by Cathal Patrick Little

An English Literature teacher living and working in Belfast, Northern Ireland. Cathal Patrick Little studied English and Philosophy at Queens University Belfast, specialising in modern existentialist literature. Little currently alternates between the cold water surf on the Irish Atlantic and Barcelona on the Mediterranean for recreation and inspiration.

Bellwether Messages

Stopping in Barcelona - July 2012

Exiled from thought and feeling,
A mean brutality reigns - Patrick Kavanagh

I was humming an old Irish song my mother taught me
"Seven long years would soon pass over,
And we'd live happy on Lough Erne's shore"
Futile memories of fishing in the cold with aims to cool.

From Mulanje's towering mountain and red dust
I had yet to return to my hometown, much nearer than
before
Yet still a long way beyond that flat, listless sea.

The road and the air are not so different;
Even the sky won't lower itself but don't we
Fool ourselves by reaching for it!

All caught between earth and air
With feet and head soaked in the Spanish sun.

I was equating myself to The Wandering Jew
Who with a taunting tongue mocked the Nazarene,
Yet wasn't he asking for it?
My sympathy can only stretch so far
For a mouthy man, or any man for that matter.

"Keep your eyes open and your mouth shut, mate!"

Yet like Jean Baptiste caught in Amsterdam's mists
I see them here, contorted with a familiar morass of
thoughts;
Did she jump or fall?
One thing we know for certain is that
The water is cold.

Weary with cold red wine and screeching white sun,
The streets heave, contract and weave around me;
They tower and fall though a relentless river of
gargoyles, tourists, temptations and Arab thieves.
Perpetual motion in action, they say.

Cervesa, aqua, coca-cola?
Cervesa, aqua, coca-cola?
Cervesa, aqua, coca-cola?
Aqui!

God knows I am conscious that the wheat needs to be tied
to the bag,
Soon or now.

A Poem by Uhene'

So being inspired by seeing the depths of God's beauty both inwardly as well as outwardly, then giving thanks and praise for it by the formulation of descriptive words flowing together. As I wander the sidewalks of Waikiki, Hawaii, on the weekend to pass out materials with a couple of buddies, it's about sharing together a belief. One day no one showed and there were no materials to pass out, so I got an idea: Instead of using materials, we could use inspirational words to say how beautiful people are among the beauty that's around, the marvelous creation. I started each resulting poem with the words "Your Beauty." Me, I was born and raised on Oahu, Hawaii. Did get the opportunity to see some other beautiful places, like Santa Cruz, California, and Charlotte, North Caroline, which I, too, amazingly love.

The beauty that is in my eyes and goes to my heart from the Marvelous Handiwork.

Dedicated to

My Dad, Robert Sr., whose absent from the body and present with the Lord, and my Mother who is here on planet earth advising the angel on my shoulder walking with me throughout this life.

My good friend Scott H. who I hang around with and is a singing sensation.

My brothers from Tuesday fellowship, cookout from Window of Hope, mighty men of God.

My brothers at my Friday night study fellowship with always something yummy to eat, Peter B., Tom S., Tom T,. Daniel, Dougy and Pastor Joe

Aloha and mahalo

The Beauty Creation of Love we See is the Love we See in it:
The Beauty of Adventure

Your beauty is as the evening shade beyond the channels
of an alluring snowflake that is perfectly and originally fit
together, each one.
So an entitlement is given proclaiming from Heaven of
such gorgeous glittering of remedy displayed.
Hush now, don't let me cry from your tender love that
you have so cherishably given unto me.
As a sign is sent down from the Heaven is that calls forth
the immaculate beauty whispering first and then
resounding triumphantly upon all creations, an
amazement of delight, as it imminently glows a crystal
shine engulfs upon my endearment of heart.
Enchantment which enhances an elite radiance of
awestruck beauty created by the Master's handiwork of
marvelous love.
This craftiness of magnificent design is majestically
woven together as it intertwines the deepest of souls
shapely manifesting the delightful love we both have for
one another.
Your beauty is tender milk of love, forever satisfying my
thirst, for it drops precious beads of everlasting desire and
quenches my pulsating heart which gives it rest, and
moments of pure ecstatic joy.

It's your natural essence of beauty which shears amazingly across the earth announcing your florescent glowing presence that lights up my life and gives it direction.

It's pathway where I follow my heart getting a heavy dose of love from your tantalizing spirit of overwhelming delight. Always your reflecting glitters in my eyes, captivated by that warm smile you so graciously cultivated, passing on, dazzles delicately and drives on dizzy as you gravitate the refreshing flow of a waterfall and wonderful colors of a rainbow upon my vulnerable innocence, influencing of harmonic melodies that only you can give to my heart.

It's unforgettable to know, it's only you that I'll caress and inspire to love the way that I do. Your beauty has penetrated my heart to give myself reason to live. Enjoy the serene surroundings that say how really special you are, and to be existing each day near your wonderful presence of delight. Always here to catch you in my arms when you fall.

It daily touches me superlatively on the hold you have upon my irresistible love moving me deeply within never could I have ever imagined to gaze upon an adorable beauty.

How you fill me up with your sweet tenderness displayed into each absorbing spirit yearning to delight in the ever-

so-forever contour of ecstatic cascading, entrenching
showcase of beauty, every time I glance your way to take
notice of you.

How roughly you grip my heart and give me wings to fly
as you lift my feet from off the ground to transcend on air
really feeling so good, the way that you love.

For you shoot a shooting star to hit at the bull's eye which
splatters and sticks directly upon my heart forever.

Your beauty is as a crystal delight of enchanting love that
displays a majestic brilliance which is seen only in your
presence the gleaming glow transferring selectively the
captivating aura, promoting clearly your sweetness of
inspiration that's given.

Cherish bountiful by the gathering of sparkling treasure
adorned upon your beauty my love, entrenches with an
assortment of imminent colors of a rainbow glistening
upon cascading flowing waterfalls that forever makes a
melody of harmonic entrenchment of magical sounds.

Let the glare of your face be transmitted exquisitely and
tantalizing blossoming starlit of unfathoming soul,
clenching wonderment that goes warmly across my heart
by the breathtaking of your voice whispering
triumphantly joyful, pleasure repulsating everlastingly a
blissful of sacred moments to eclipse and intertwine
deliverance of ravishing lovely beauty.

Your beauty is overwhelmingly going beyond measure
with your extremely gorgeous smile that captives me.

How I so desire you, wanting so desperately to touch you gently and taste the sweetness of your dripping repelling audacious love.

Melts unequivocally in spiral array to cast unfathomable cascading fulfillment in my life as the melody of your majestic touch sends a chorus of angelic sound to my vibrating heart that whispers inspirations of deep forever everythings as I polish out my quenching desire that is thirsting for delightful love and so hoping to tuck away your sweet aroma in a crystal ball to keep my lasting love forever of you with me.

For my keen desire collides upon your glistening beauty as we came alongside each other to ravish off a combustion of energy that wants to completely lead you directly to the steps of Heaven's gate because there is no better way to Heaven by which true beauty originates and I have found someone so wonderfully beautiful as yourself.

Bellwether Messages

A Poem by Peter Mallett

Peter Mallett is an award winning photographer who has recently become interested in writing as an additional creative outlet. "My work is often reflective and metaphorical. I seek a way to connect inner experience with outer reality. Poetry offers a way to blend both in a meaningfully succinct way."

He currently resides in Hawaii on the island of Oahu.

Bellwether Messages

Realization

Two a.m.
Jive talk, syncopated conversation
A hooker at the corner
strikes a pose near the lamp post
"Wanna date" she calls
The old man laughs
and turns his head

Stragglers begin to empty the bars
Those who never had a chance
to find another
and share their misery
He watches them one by one
turn a collar up
wrap a coat
The night air is cold

The old man remembers
He was was once young and empty

Searching for some meaning
Some thread
To hold his life together

Then one day he found God
in a moment of inattention
A revelation out of the blue
He found God
in the hooker
and the stragglers
and his own inconsequential life

Bellwether Messages

Three Poems by Tender Bastard

Author, playwright, performing-songwriter, Tender Bastard (Scott Mastro) is an artist whose bank statement affirms his credentials. Current projects include the CD/DVD *Word of Mouth*, the play *Moon Over Mangroves*, a satirical historical-fiction series entitled *Sticks and Stones* and a sleuth series featuring *Thelonius Thunderbird Merlot*, a moron with a moral compass.

Without creativity and the muses, this poet wouldn't know what to do with his life. As a child, he dreamed of being all Three Stooges; that has gladly since changed. Instead he authored a short story collection, BLOOD MONEY: TALES FROM TWO CONTINENTS (Savant 2012). When not writing and performing, he plays with his dog.

Bellwether Messages

Rooftop of the La Concha

The sun's going down,
like the sun always does,
but will it be coming tomorrow?

I know that it has,
but a lot of bad jazz
has brought many complete ruin and sorrow.

The world hasn't ended
as the Mayans intended,
not even way back in 2000,

So let's all drink up,
and then we can sup,
in Paradise - stop all your grousin.'

Will I be seeing you,
where this town's only view
looks out over the gulf and the ocean?

Where something un-planned
might turn out really grand.
without need for suntanning lotion.

I am trying to do
something good in this world
just like the Man of La Mancha.
If the world has to end,
I'll see you, my friend,
on the *Rooftop of the La Concha.*

In the world of finance,
I will not wear the pants.
I never will be a big honcho.
But when the sun's going down,
you know I'll be found, on the *Rooftop of the La Concha.*

So lift up your cocktail.
Let the music play on.
I'll go down with the ship like a man
On the *Rooftop of the La Concha* Hotel.
Where Culture is still in demand.

Some people pronounce it, La Konka.
They don't know what they're talking about.

What some people say,
and some people do,
fills me with heart-piercing doubt.

And I know that this world can be brutal,

the gut-wrenching lessons it gives.
The La Concha roof,
supplies ample proof,
that genuine Decency lives.

The Titanic went down,
and the Hindenburg blew,
I know that someday it all ends.
On the *Rooftop of the La Concha* Hotel
I feel love of both strangers and friends.

And I'm thankful that I can be singing, look at this
fabulous view that we've found
On the *Rooftop of the La Concha* Hotel, seven stories
above the cruel ground.

And at least for the moment,
we're grateful to know it,
all might someday turn out well.

There is no other place
on this earth's brilliant face
like the *Rooftop of the La Concha* Hotel.

No place to be,
except here with me,
on the *Rooftop of the La Concha* Hotel.

Bellwether Messages

Asshole O'clock

If you ever get down to Bone Island
and stroll Duval Street, any block
Between 11 at night and 1 in the morning,
it's ASSHOLE O'CLOCK.

Its own international time zone,
from around the world people flock
To be on Duval between 11 and 1
for ASSHOLE O'CLOCK.

Like everyone punching a time card announcing
that they've showed up for work
Or someone blowing a whistle to signal,
"It's time to start being a jerk."

It's written in every tour guide book,
so it shouldn't come as a shock,
On Duval Street between 11 and 1,
it's ASSHOLE O'CLOCK.

The harbor's jammed with ocean liners,
all of them tryna' dock
so everybody can get to Duval Street
when it's ASSHOLE O'CLOCK.

Boat people comin' from Cuba,
risking their lives to get on this rock,
writing home to say they made it on time
for ASSHOLE O'CLOCK.

A couple of friends came down in hopes
of having a nice vacation.
They were on Duval for ASSHOLE O'CLOCK
and went home on probation.

Let this be a lesson to all.
It ain't no bunch of crock.
Something happens to people on Duval Street
when it's ASSHOLE O'CLOCK.

The little hand's on the eleven.
The big hand's standing up straight.
ASSHOLE O'CLOCK is just getting started.
Which asshole will officiate
as the master of ceremonies over all of the assholes
in the place they congregate
from 11 to 1, it's ASSHOLE O'CLOCK,
on Duval; let's celebrate.

You'd have to be an asshole
to miss out on the fun.
If you're on Duval between those two hours,

you might be the biggest one.

No can of beans or chunk of baloney,
not even a smokin' ham hock.
Duval is where assholes pursue
their art at ASSHOLE O'CLOCK.

As if a magic comes over the place,
in one hickory-dickory dock,
raging, ranting, babbling nitwits
all chime in at ASSHOLE O'CLOCK.

There must be a passport, some temporary I.D.
that can be acquired ad-hoc,
making everyone honorary members
of ASSHOLE O'CLOCK.

From Sloppy Joe's Bar to Bourbon Street Pub
and all the way up to Aqua.
Between 11 and 1 on Duval each night,
it ain't no Chautauqua.

And that's what makes this country so great,
the unfettered freedom to walk
down Duval Street between 11 and 1
for ASSHOLE OCLOCK.

It brings out the best and the worst of the soul,
even priests and nuns will de-frock
on Duval Street between 11 and 1,
it's ASSHOLE O'CLOCK.

Super Hero

Everybody needs a super hero – someone to save the day
It doesn't matter if you can fly or shoot a super ray
You just have to be there whenever you're needed
And always be a friend
A SUPER HERO right to the end

When there's trouble – on the double – you quickly sort
things out
Leave no one hanging – Leave no one in doubt
That you're good for your word
And you'll do what you say
And you'll always lend a hand
That's how a SUPER HERO's day is planned

You've met every obstacle
And you've worked to tear them down
You've climbed the mountain
And turned this game around
Lied to and cheated,
Nearly defeated,
You've reached down deep inside
And given one more SUPER HERO try

Everybody's a SUPER HERO, if they can just be true

Look around and you'll see somebody who thinks that
way of you
Swing for the fence,
Keep your head held high,
And strive for an ideal
We'll all be SUPER HEROes
Raw-raw-siss-boom-baw, not zeroes
We'll all be SUPER HEROes for real.

Bellwether Messages

Three Poems by Emma Myles

Emma Myles is a creative person who finds inspiration in the world around her. Her favorite poem is *The Bells*, by Edgar Allan Poe. Originally from California, Miss Myles currently resides in Hawaii.

ACORNS

See them lying on their leafy mats,
As if dressed up in Russian hats;
Yet the snowy hills are not their domain,
The only exciting thing is rain.

They come in colors brown and green,
They have no Prince, nor King nor Queen;
Yet they are the noblest of forest folk,
They love to dance and sing and joke.

They throw balls just like royalty,
And dress up right royally.
Across the forest floor they glide,
All dancing together side-by-side.

They trip and roll over leaves,
Never dirtying their lovely sleeves.
Oh yes! How grand it must be!
The royal forest folk to see.

OVER THE HILLSIDE

Over the hillside
An army charges on
A thousand horse hooves
Pounding
Thunderous and strong.

Ahead rides Truth.
His sword glimmers in the light.
He's come to break down the wrong
And uphold the right.
Courage leads his army,
With never faltering heart.
And Love upon her horse of red
Clasps her heart-shaped dart.

Peace looks serene
Upon her horse of white
And Justice, upon his horse of black
Looks as stately as a knight.
Hope and Perseverance ride side-by-side
Gallantly pounding through the countryside

As a living sea they charge
To the castle gate
They knock the dreadful fortress down

Their weapon is love not hate.

As victors they turn
triumphantly
Toward home.
As they gallop cheerfully
Along a babbling brook.
Presently they come,
To a sun filled nook
They stop for a drink
and to rest awhile.
As they gaze into the sky
They think
And smile.

PICTURES IN THE SKY

See the clouds up in the sky
How they swirl!
How they twirl!
And how gracefully they curl
Through the sky!

See them drifting,
See them shifting
Just to watch is so uplifting!
As they flutter and they float
Like the sails upon a boat.

See them race!
See them glide!
On the wind do they ride!
Sailing on, on, on
On the ocean of the sky.

As they lazily roll by
They paint pictures in the sky
Of boats and birds and bats
And of pampered Siamese cats.
Sitting peacefully on their seats
Up in the sky.

Puffs of cotton
Wisps of wool,
like string upon a spool
How they twist and turn and fly
On their canvas
In the sky.

See them twisting!
See them twirling!
And how haphazardly they're curling
As though they're swirling
And they're spiraling
Through the sky!

And we watch in rapt delight
Until the coming of the night
As they run and race and play
Then they're gone!

For the wind, so pushy,
Pushes them along
Without a word or a song
Just pushes them along
Blowing and flowing
Not knowing where it's going
Just blows.

And the fluffy, puffy clouds,
Without a care or a worry,
So not in a hurry,
Just goes.

A Poem by Ken Rasti

Ken Rasti, also known as "Yes" among friends, is a Professor at several universities and a business management consultant for multiple organizations. He recently was inducted into the Heroes of Humanity Hall of Fame in recognition of his many positive community contributions with Aloha in the Heart Center. He recently had a prose article published titled, "Aloha, I Love You, *We Are All Connected*", in a book titled *Messages of Peace*. He lives in Hawaii, and has a daughter and a son who live and work in California.

My daughter, Mitrah Rasti, and my son, Dimitri Rasti

Aloha, I Love You:
We Are All Connected

Connection
Universal Energy
Gracious, Life-Giving Mother Earth

We are all connected
Strong and humble trees
whose leaves dance gently in the breeze
Encompassing expansive sky
her child-winds, our magical energy
Ever-abundant deep-blue ocean
connecting all through liquid love.

Visiting the ocean in Hawaii
as I often do when troubled
returns to me my sense of Aloha
I ask her permission to wash my troubles away in her
She always welcomes me sweetly with gentleness
in five shades of blue
Her majestic beauty refills my heart
with joy, love, peace
She changes my focus
from my troubles to my blessings
to gratitude

a magical shift
the leaves in its wake
peace, connectedness, love, acceptance.

Helpless to create harmony in my life
fears and apprehensions surrounding
Meditate Aloha
Meditate patience and kindness
in the arms of Mother Earth
is the key to serenity.

Breath
Forgive
Be childlike
Laugh
Allow happiness to steep into every niche
Say yes
Say Aloha
I love you
We are all connected.

Bellwether Messages

Three Poems by Ashley Vaughan

Ashley Vaughan is a southern girl, raised in Columbia, South Carolina. After living in Honolulu, Hawai'i, and Tautu, Vanuatu (SW Pacific), she developed a deep respect for indigenous Pacific Island cultures. These experiences have allowed her to combine her loves of anthropology, research, academic writing, and creative writing. Ashley holds a B.A. in anthropology and English from the University of South Carolina and a PhD. in anthropology from the University of Hawai'i at Manoa. The rest is a secret, for now, as she wishes to remain slightly mysterious.

For my parents, for always being there and for
introducing me to the Pacific Ocean.

Against aquarium glass

Ten feet above the water,
and it's still like pressing
against aquarium glass—
the blue and the bubbles—
so clear I can taste it,
I could maybe even drink it.
So clear it could maybe even
quench this dizzy thirst.
So clear it could maybe even
fill the flask where
my heart used to be.
It could maybe even
be better than
tequila,
vodka,
your love.

For anyone who has ever been left hanging.

Hanging out to dry

My skin is chapped
from the washing,
from the perfumed
powdered soap.
My hands are sore
from wringing
out the water.
I rinse.
I wring.
I think of you,
and I try to
squeeze out
the disappointment.
I try to picture
my sadness fading
like sweat stains
sucked dry by
the scorching
Vanuatu sun.

For the unsatisfied.

Sweet potato (stuffed)

Sometimes prickly
(but mostly) pure
hardy pleasure.
Peel me.
Warm me up.
One bite can
nourish you like no other,
can placate that homewrecker
hunger, that too familiar emptiness,
that growling, unruly ennui.
Look at me:
peeled, purple,
undone.
Your eyes are always
bigger than
your heart.
Just finish me already.
Just fucking finish me.

First Breath - 2010 Savant Anthology of Poems (2010)
Zachary M. Oliver (Editor)
72 pp. 8.25" x 5" Softcover
ISBN 978-0-9845552-2-2

Twenty-nine poems by ten outstanding poets and writers selected for their outstanding merit, including Helen Doan, Erin L. George, Jack Howard, Daniel S. Janik, Scott Mastro, Zachary M. Oliver, Francis H. Powell, Gabjirel Ra, V. Bright Saigal and Orest Stocco.

Wavelengths - 2011 Savant Poetry Anthology (2011)
Zachary M. Oliver (Editor)
102 pp; 5.25" x 8" Softcover
ISBN 978-0-9829987-6-2

Thirty-eight poems by sixteen outstanding poets and writers
including Four Arrows, Penny Lynn Cates, J. R. Coleman,
Nadia Cox, Helen Doan, Erin L George, IKO, Daniel S. Janik,
Vivekanand Jha, A. K. Kelly, Zachary M. Oliver, Cara
Richardson, Michael Shorb, Jason Sturner, Jean Yamasaki
Toyama and Jeremy Ussher.

LONDON BOOK FESTIVAL AWARD

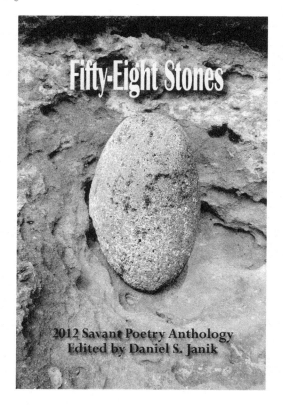

Fifty-Eight Stones - 2012 Savant Poetry Anthology (2012)
Daniel S. Janik (Editor)
128 pp. - 5.25" x 8" Softcover
ISBN 978-0-9852506-5-2

Thirty-four outstanding poems by eleven exceptional and many award-winning poets including Shawn Canon, Nadia Cox, Helen Doan, David Gemmell, Richard Hookway, Daniel S. Janik, Vivekanand Jha, Doc Krinberg, Julie McKinney, Francis Powell and Jean Yamasaki Toyama.

If you enjoyed *Bellwether Messages,* consider these other fine works from Savant Books and Publications:

Savant Poetry Anthologies:
***First Breath* (2010) edited by Z. M. Oliver**
***Wavelengths* (2011) edited by Zachary M. Oliver**
***Fifty-Eight Stones* (2012) edited by Daniel S. Janik**

Other Savant Poetry Collections:
Footprints, Smiles and Little White Lies by Daniel S. Janik
The Illustrated Middle Earth by Daniel S. Janik
Last and Final Harvest by Daniel S. Janik

Other Savant Books and Publications:
Essay, Essay, Essay by Ysuo Kobachi
A Whale's Tale by Daniel S. Janik
Tropic of California by R. Page Kaufman
Tropic of California (the companion music CD) by R. Page Kaufman
The Village Curtain by Tony Tame
Dare to Love in Oz by William Maltese
The Interzone by Tatsuyuki Kobayashi
Today I Am a Man by Larry Rodness
The Bahrain Conspiracy by Bentley Gates
Called Home by Gloria Schumann
Kanaka Blues by Mike Farris
Poor Rich by Jean Blasiar
The Jumper Chronicles - Quest for Merlin's Map by W. C. Peever
William Maltese's Flicker by William Maltese
My Unborn Child by Orest Stocco
Last Song of the Whales by Four Arrows
Perilous Panacea by Ronald Klueh
Falling but Fulfilled by Zachary M. Oliver
Mythical Voyage by Robin Ymer
Hello, Norma Jean by Sue Dolleris
Richer by Jean Blasiar
Manifest Intent by Mike Farris
Charlie No Face by David B. Seaburn

Number One Bestseller by Brian Morley
My Two Wives and Three Husbands by S. Stanley Gordon
In Dire Straits by Jim Currie
Wretched Land by Mila Komarnisky
Chan Kim by Ilan Herman
Who's Killing All the Lawyers? by A. G. Hayes
Ammon's Horn by G. Amati
Almost Paradise by Laurie Hanan
Communion by Jean Blasiar and Jonathan Marcantoni
The Oil Man by Leon Puissegur
Random Views of Asia from the Mid-Pacific by William E. Sharp
The Isla Vista Crucible by Reilly Ridgell
Blood Money by Scott Mastro
In the Himalayan Nights by Anoop Chandola
Rules of Privilege by Mike Farris
On My Behalf by Helen Doan
Traveler's Rest by Jonathan Marcantoni
Keys in the River by Tendai Mwanaka
Chimney Bluffs by David B. Seaburn
The Loons by Sue Dolleris
The Judas List by A. G. Hayes
Path of the Templar - Book Two of The Jumper Chronicles by W. C. Peever
Shutterbug by Buz Sawyers
The Desperate Cycle by Tony Tame
Blessed are the Peacekeepers by Tom Donnelly and Mike Munger

Soon to be Released:
The Lazarus Conspiracies by Richard Rose
The Hanging of Dr. Hanson by Bentley Gates
Purple Haze by George B. Hudson

www.savantbooksandpublications.com
www.savantbookstorehonolulu.com

127

TO MORGANSTEIN
                 OHANA

MAY THE REFLECTIVE
LIGHT OF THE HEAVENS
BRING A GUIDANCE
OF TOUCH IN THE
    JOURNEY OF THE
PATHWAY, TO TOUCH
MANY LIVES. AS
MANY FIND THEIR
WAYS HOME

Made in the USA
Columbia, SC
19 November 2020

E pule u fani oé
    PRAYER FROM
    HEAVEN TO
    YOU.
            UHENE
                 S

24902149R00075